Table Of Contents

- Definition of Mindset Mastery 2
- Importance of Overcoming Self-Doubt 2
- Overview of Chapters 2
- The Power of Mindset 2
  - Understanding the Mindset of Successful Entrepreneurs 2
  - The Role of Self-Doubt in Limiting Success 2
  - The Science of Mindset: Neuroplasticity and Growth Mindset 2
- Identifying Self-Doubt 2
  - Understanding the Root Causes of Self-Doubt 2
  - Recognizing Self-Limiting Beliefs 2
  - Overcoming Imposter Syndrome 2
- Building a Strong Mindset 2
  - Developing a Strong Personal Vision 2
  - Building Resilience and Grit 2
  - The Power of Positive Affirmations 2
- Practicing Mindfulness 2
  - Understanding Mindfulness and Its Benefits 2
  - Mindfulness Techniques for Entrepreneurs 2
  - Using Mindfulness to Overcome Self-Doubt 2
- Developing a Growth Mindset 2
  - Understanding the Difference between Fixed and Growth Mindset 2
  - How to Develop a Growth Mindset 2
  - The Benefits of a Growth Mindset for Entrepreneurs 2
- Overcoming Failure and Setbacks 2
  - Understanding Failure and Resilience 2
  - Learning from Failure and Moving Forward 2
  - Overcoming Setbacks and Challenges 2
- Navigating the Entrepreneurial Journey 2
  - The Importance of Goal Setting 2
  - Staying Focused and Motivated 2
  - Embracing Change and Managing Uncertainty 2
- Conclusion 2

Recap of Key Takeaways 2
Final Thoughts and Encouragement 2
Resources for Further Learning and Growth. 2
Introduction 1

Introduction

Definition of Mindset Mastery

and "Achieving Success".

Definition of Mindset Mastery

As an entrepreneur, your mindset is your most valuable asset. How you think and feel about yourself and your business can make or break your success. Mindset mastery is the process of taking control of your thoughts, beliefs, and attitudes so that they work in your favor. It's about cultivating a positive, growth-oriented mindset that allows you to overcome self-doubt, push past obstacles, and achieve your goals.

At the heart of mindset mastery is the belief that your mind is a powerful tool that you can learn to use to your advantage. Your thoughts and beliefs shape your reality, so if you want to change your reality, you must first change your mindset. This means becoming aware of your limiting beliefs and negative thought patterns and replacing them with positive, empowering ones.

Mindset mastery is not a one-time event but an ongoing process. It requires discipline, commitment, and a willingness to do the inner work required to create lasting change. It's not always easy, but the rewards are well worth it. When you have a strong, resilient mindset, you can face any challenge with confidence and resilience.

One of the keys to mindset mastery is learning to embrace failure as a necessary part of the learning process. Failure is not a reflection of your worth or ability, but simply a stepping stone on the path to success. When you can reframe failure as an opportunity for growth and learning, you take away its power to hold you back.

Another important aspect of mindset mastery is developing a growth mindset. This means believing that your abilities and intelligence can be developed through hard work and dedication. With a growth mindset, you see challenges as opportunities to learn and grow, rather than as threats to your self-esteem.

Again, mindset mastery is about taking control of your thoughts, beliefs, and attitudes so that they work in your favor. It's about cultivating a positive, growth-oriented mindset that allows you to overcome self-doubt, push past obstacles, and achieve your goals. With mindset mastery, you can become the best version of yourself and create the success you desire.

Importance of Overcoming Self-Doubt

As an entrepreneur, self-doubt is something that can creep up at any moment. It's that voice in the back of your head that tells you that you're not good enough, that you're not smart enough, or that you're not capable of achieving success. The problem with self-doubt is that it can hold you back from achieving your full potential as an entrepreneur. It can stop you from taking risks, trying new things, and pursuing your dreams.

Overcoming self-doubt is essential if you want to succeed as an entrepreneur. Here are a few reasons why:

1. Self-doubt can hold you back from taking risks.

As an entrepreneur, taking risks is essential. You need to be willing to try new things, experiment with different strategies, and take bold steps to grow your business. However, self-doubt can stop you from taking those risks. It can make you hesitant and fearful, causing you to miss out on opportunities that could have been game-changers for your business.

2. Self-doubt can limit your creativity.

As an entrepreneur, creativity is key. You need to be able to think outside the box, come up with innovative solutions, and find new ways to stand out from the competition. However, self-doubt can limit your creativity. It can make you second-guess your ideas, causing you to play it safe and stick with what's familiar.

3. Self-doubt can damage your confidence.

Confidence is crucial for success as an entrepreneur. You need to believe in yourself and your abilities if you want others to believe in you too. However, self-doubt can damage your confidence. It can make you doubt your skills and talents, causing you to feel insecure and unsure of yourself.

4. Self-doubt can limit your success.

Ultimately, self-doubt can limit your success as an entrepreneur. It can hold you back from achieving your goals and reaching your full potential. It can stop you from taking the actions you need to take to grow your business and achieve your dreams.

Overcoming self-doubt is not easy, but it's essential if you want to succeed as an entrepreneur. It requires you to believe in yourself, trust your instincts, and take action despite your fears. It's about recognizing that self-doubt is just a voice in your head, and it doesn't have to control your actions or limit your success.

In the next chapter, we'll explore some practical strategies for overcoming self-doubt and achieving success as an entrepreneur. From changing your mindset to building your confidence, these strategies will help you overcome self-doubt and achieve your full potential as an entrepreneur.

Target Audience: Entrepreneurs

and "Achieving Success".

Entrepreneurs are a unique group of individuals who possess a drive and determination that is unmatched in any other profession. However, this drive can sometimes be accompanied by self-doubt, which can ultimately hinder their success. To overcome self-doubt and achieve success, entrepreneurs must develop a mindset that is focused on growth and continuous improvement.

One of the first steps that entrepreneurs can take towards developing a growth mindset is to identify their target audience. Entrepreneurs must have a clear understanding of who their product or service is intended for, and they must tailor their marketing efforts accordingly. By understanding their target audience, entrepreneurs can identify their pain points and offer solutions that are tailored to their specific needs.

Another important aspect of developing a growth mindset is to embrace failure. Entrepreneurs must understand that failure is a natural part of the learning process, and that every failure is an opportunity to learn and grow. By embracing failure and learning from their mistakes, entrepreneurs can refine their strategies and improve their chances of success.

In addition to embracing failure, entrepreneurs must also be persistent in their pursuit of success. Success rarely comes overnight, and entrepreneurs must be willing to put in the time and effort required to achieve their goals. This requires a high level of commitment and dedication, as well as the ability to stay focused and motivated even in the face of setbacks.

Ultimately, the key to overcoming self-doubt and achieving success as an entrepreneur is to develop a growth mindset that is focused on continuous improvement. By understanding their target audience, embracing failure, and staying persistent in their pursuit of success, entrepreneurs can overcome the challenges that come with starting a new business and achieve their goals. With the right mindset and approach, entrepreneurs can turn their dreams into reality and make a lasting impact in their industry.

Overview of Chapters

and "Achieving Success".

The journey to becoming a successful entrepreneur is not an easy one. It requires hard work, dedication, and a mindset that is geared towards achieving success. In this book, we will explore the different chapters that are designed to help you overcome self-doubt and achieve success.

Chapter 1: The Power of Mindset

The first chapter of the book is all about understanding the power of mindset. It explores the different types of mindsets that entrepreneurs have and how they can impact their success. We will also discuss the importance of having a growth mindset and how it can help you overcome self-doubt.

Chapter 2: Overcoming Self-Doubt

Self-doubt is one of the biggest obstacles that entrepreneurs face. In this chapter, we will explore the different ways in which you can overcome self-doubt. We will also discuss the importance of self-confidence and how it can help you achieve success.

Chapter 3: Setting Goals and Creating a Plan

Setting goals and creating a plan is crucial to achieving success. In this chapter, we will discuss the different types of goals that entrepreneurs can set and how to create a plan that will help you achieve those goals.

Chapter 4: Taking Action

Taking action is the key to achieving success. In this chapter, we will explore the different actions that entrepreneurs can take to achieve success. We will also discuss the importance of persistence and how it can help you overcome obstacles.

Chapter 5: Building a Support System

Building a support system is crucial for entrepreneurs. In this chapter, we will explore the different types of support systems that entrepreneurs can build and how they can help you overcome self-doubt and achieve success.

Chapter 6: Staying Motivated

Staying motivated is crucial to achieving success. In this chapter, we will explore the different ways in which you can stay motivated and focused on your goals.

In conclusion, this book is designed to help entrepreneurs overcome self-doubt and achieve success. By exploring the different chapters, you will gain the knowledge and tools that you need to develop a mindset that is geared towards achieving the success, happiness and life that you desire.

The Power of Mindset

Understanding the Mindset of Successful Entrepreneurs

and "Achieving Success".

In order to become a successful entrepreneur, it is essential to understand the mindset of successful entrepreneurs. This mindset is not something that comes naturally to everyone, but it can be learned and developed over time with the right mindset mastery techniques.

One of the key characteristics of a successful entrepreneur is the ability to take risks. Entrepreneurs who are willing to take calculated risks are often the ones who achieve the greatest success. However, taking risks can be a daunting prospect for many people, particularly those who struggle with self-doubt. Overcoming self-doubt is therefore essential if you want to develop the mindset of a successful entrepreneur.

Another important characteristic of successful entrepreneurs is their ability to think outside of the box. Successful entrepreneurs are often able to see opportunities where others see only obstacles. They are able to think creatively and come up with innovative solutions to problems. This requires a certain level of mental flexibility and adaptability, as well as the ability to think critically.

Successful entrepreneurs also tend to be highly driven and motivated. They are passionate about their work and are willing to put in the time and effort required to achieve their goals. This requires a certain level of discipline and focus, as well as the ability to prioritize tasks and manage time effectively.

Finally, successful entrepreneurs are often highly resilient. They are able to bounce back from setbacks and failures, and are able to learn from their mistakes. This requires a certain level of emotional intelligence and the ability to manage stress and anxiety effectively.

Developing the mindset of a successful entrepreneur takes time and effort, but it is possible for anyone who is willing to put in the work. By overcoming self-doubt, thinking creatively, staying motivated and focused, and being resilient in the face of setbacks, you can develop the mindset of a successful entrepreneur and achieve great success in your business endeavors.

The Role of Self-Doubt in Limiting Success

Self-doubt is a common feeling that often creeps up on entrepreneurs, especially during difficult times or when taking a big risk. It can be crippling, leading to inaction, self-sabotage, and missed opportunities. In this subchapter, we will explore the role of self-doubt in limiting success and how to overcome it.

Firstly, it's important to understand that self-doubt is a natural part of the human experience. We all have moments of uncertainty and fear, and it's okay to feel that way. However, when self-doubt becomes a persistent thought pattern, it can hold us back from achieving our goals.

One of the main ways self-doubt limits success is by creating a negative mindset. When we doubt ourselves, we start to believe that we are not capable of achieving our goals. This negative self-talk can become a self-fulfilling prophecy, leading us to give up before even trying. To overcome this, it's important to recognize when negative thoughts are creeping in and replace them with positive self-talk. Instead of saying "I can't do this," try saying "I am capable of achieving this."

Another way self-doubt limits success is by causing us to second-guess our decisions. When we doubt ourselves, we may hesitate to take action or make decisions, leading to missed opportunities. To overcome this, it's important to trust your instincts and make decisions based on your goals and values.

Remember that failure is a natural part of the entrepreneurial journey and that every failure is an opportunity to learn and grow.

Lastly, self-doubt can limit success by causing us to compare ourselves to others. When we doubt ourselves, we may feel inferior to others and believe that we will never measure up. To overcome this, it's important to focus on your own journey and progress rather than comparing yourself to others. Remember that everyone has their own unique path to success, and comparing yourself to others will only hold you back.

Self-doubt can be a significant obstacle to success for entrepreneurs. By recognizing the negative thought patterns that self-doubt creates and replacing them with positive self-talk, trusting your instincts and making decisions based on your goals and values, and focusing on your own journey rather than comparing yourself to others, you can overcome self-doubt and achieve success. Remember that mindset mastery is a journey, and it takes practice and commitment to overcome self-doubt and achieve your goals.

The Science of Mindset: Neuroplasticity and Growth Mindset

and "Achieving Success".

The Science of Mindset: Neuroplasticity and Growth Mindset

As an entrepreneur, your mindset plays a vital role in your success. The way you think and perceive things can either hinder or propel you towards achieving your goals. The good news is that the brain is malleable and can be rewired for success. This is where the science of mindset comes in, particularly neuroplasticity and growth mindset.

Neuroplasticity refers to the brain's ability to change and adapt throughout your life. It was once believed that the brain stops growing and developing after childhood, but recent studies have shown that it can continue to grow and change, depending on the experiences and activities you engage in. This means that you have the power to rewire your brain to think and act in ways that are more conducive to success.

Growth mindset, on the other hand, is the belief that your intelligence, abilities, and talents can be developed through hard work, dedication, and learning from mistakes. It is the opposite of a fixed mindset, which believes that your qualities are fixed and cannot be changed. People with a growth mindset see challenges as opportunities to learn and grow, while those with a fixed mindset see them as threats to their abilities and self-worth.

Studies have shown that people with a growth mindset are more likely to take on challenges, persist in the face of setbacks, and achieve their goals. They also have a greater sense of resilience and are less likely to be held back by self-doubt and limiting beliefs.

So, how can you develop a growth mindset and take advantage of neuroplasticity? Here are some tips:

1. Embrace challenges - instead of avoiding challenges or giving up at the first sign of difficulty, see them as opportunities to learn and grow.

2. Learn from mistakes - don't be afraid to make mistakes, as they are a natural part of the learning process. Instead, use them as opportunities to learn and improve.

3. Focus on the process - instead of just focusing on the end result, focus on the steps you need to take to get there. This will help you stay motivated and committed to your goals.

4. Surround yourself with positivity - surround yourself with people who have a growth mindset and who will support and encourage you on your journey.

By developing a growth mindset and taking advantage of neuroplasticity, you can overcome self-doubt and achieve success as an entrepreneur. Remember, your mindset is a powerful tool, so use it wisely.

Identifying Self-Doubt

Understanding the Root Causes of Self-Doubt

Understanding the Root Causes of Self-Doubt

Self-doubt can be a significant barrier to success for entrepreneurs. It can hold you back from taking risks, pursuing opportunities, and achieving your goals. However, the good news is that by understanding the root causes of self-doubt, you can begin to overcome it.

One of the primary causes of self-doubt is fear of failure. The fear of failure can be paralyzing and can make you question your abilities and worth. However, it's essential to understand that failure is a part of the entrepreneurial journey. Not everything you try will work, and that's okay. The key is to learn from your failures and use them as opportunities for growth and development.

Another root cause of self-doubt is the imposter syndrome. The imposter syndrome is the feeling that you're not qualified, experienced, or talented enough to be doing what you're doing. It can lead to a lack of confidence and feelings of inadequacy. However, it's important to remember that everyone experiences self-doubt at some point, and it doesn't mean you're not capable or qualified.

Comparing yourself to others is another common cause of self-doubt. It's easy to get caught up in comparing your progress, successes, and failures to those of others. However, this can be detrimental to your self-esteem and confidence. Instead, focus on your own journey and progress and celebrate your successes, no matter how small.

Lastly, a lack of clarity and direction can also lead to self-doubt. If you're unsure of what you want to achieve or how to get there, it can be challenging to have confidence in yourself and your abilities. Take the time to set clear goals and develop a plan for achieving them. This will help you stay focused and motivated, and ultimately boost your confidence and self-belief.

Understanding the root causes of self-doubt is essential for overcoming it. By recognizing and addressing these causes, you can develop a more positive mindset and increase your confidence and self-belief. Remember, self-doubt is a natural part of the entrepreneurial journey, but it doesn't have to hold you back. With the right mindset and strategies, you can overcome it and achieve success.

Recognizing Self-Limiting Beliefs

and "Achieving Success".

Recognizing Self-Limiting Beliefs

As an entrepreneur, our mindset plays a crucial role in our success. Our beliefs, both positive and negative, shape our decisions, actions, and outcomes. However, not all beliefs are empowering. Some beliefs can be self-limiting and hold us back from achieving our full potential. These beliefs are often deeply ingrained and may have been formed in our childhood or past experiences.

Recognizing self-limiting beliefs is the first step towards overcoming them. Here are some common self-limiting beliefs that entrepreneurs may face:

1. "I'm not good enough": This belief is a common one that can hold us back from taking risks or pursuing our goals. We may doubt our abilities and feel like we're not qualified enough to succeed.

2. "I don't have enough resources": This belief can make us feel like we don't have the necessary time, money, or connections to achieve our goals. We may feel like we're stuck and can't move forward.

3. "I'm too old/young": Age can be a limiting factor for some entrepreneurs. Older entrepreneurs may feel like they're past their prime, while younger entrepreneurs may feel like they don't have enough experience.

4. "I'm not lucky": This belief can make us feel like success is based on luck, and we have no control over our outcomes.

5. "I can't handle failure": Fear of failure can hold us back from taking risks and pursuing our goals. We may feel like failure is a reflection of our abilities or worth.

Recognizing these beliefs is the first step towards overcoming them. Once we become aware of these beliefs, we can challenge them and replace them with more empowering ones. Here are some strategies for overcoming self-limiting beliefs:

1. Challenge your beliefs: Ask yourself if your beliefs are true or if they're based on assumptions or past experiences. Look for evidence to support or refute your beliefs.

2. Reframe your beliefs: Instead of focusing on what you can't do, focus on what you can do. Replace self-limiting beliefs with empowering ones that will motivate you to take action.

3. Take action: The best way to overcome self-doubt is to take action. Start small and build momentum. Celebrate your successes and learn from your failures.

Recognizing self-limiting beliefs is the first step towards achieving mindset mastery. By challenging our beliefs and replacing them with more empowering ones, we can overcome self-doubt and achieve success as entrepreneurs.

Overcoming Imposter Syndrome

and "Achieving Success."

As an entrepreneur, it can be challenging to push forward with your goals and ambitions when you're constantly struggling with imposter syndrome. You may feel like you're not good enough, that you're not qualified for the job, or that you're just lucky to be where you are. These thoughts can be paralyzing and prevent you from taking the necessary steps to achieve success.

Fortunately, there are ways to overcome imposter syndrome and move forward with confidence. Here are some strategies that can help:

1. Recognize imposter syndrome for what it is.

Imposter syndrome is a common phenomenon, affecting people from all walks of life. It's not an indication of your worth or abilities, but rather a result of the human tendency to focus on negative thoughts and self-doubt. Once you recognize that imposter syndrome is just a passing feeling, you can begin to work on overcoming it.

2. Acknowledge your achievements.

One of the most effective ways to combat imposter syndrome is to focus on your achievements. Take time to reflect on your successes, no matter how small they may seem. Write them down and remind yourself of them when imposter syndrome starts to take hold. This can help you see that you are capable of achieving great things.

3. Embrace your mistakes.

Everyone makes mistakes, and as an entrepreneur, you're likely to make plenty of them. Instead of letting mistakes feed your imposter syndrome, embrace them as learning opportunities. Use them to improve your skills and strategies, and remember that failure is a necessary step on the road to success.

4. Seek support.

It can be helpful to talk to others about imposter syndrome and seek support from those who understand what you're going through. Consider joining a support group or seeking out a mentor who can provide guidance and encouragement.

5. Practice self-compassion.

Finally, it's important to practice self-compassion as you work to overcome imposter syndrome. Be kind to yourself and remember that you are doing the best you can with the resources you have. Treat yourself with the same care and understanding that you would offer to a friend or loved one.

By recognizing imposter syndrome, acknowledging your achievements, embracing your mistakes, seeking support, and practicing self-compassion, you can overcome imposter syndrome and achieve the success you deserve as an entrepreneur. With these strategies in place, you can move forward with confidence and achieve your goals.

Building a Strong Mindset

Developing a Strong Personal Vision

and "Achieving Success".

Developing a Strong Personal Vision

In order to achieve success as an entrepreneur, it is crucial to have a strong and clear personal vision. Developing a personal vision involves understanding what you want to achieve, defining your values and beliefs, and setting goals that align with your vision.

The first step in developing a personal vision is to identify what you want to achieve. This could be a long-term goal, such as building a successful business, or a short-term goal, such as launching a new product. Whatever your goal may be, it is important to have a clear understanding of what you want to achieve and why it is important to you.

Once you have identified your goal, it is important to define your values and beliefs. Your values and beliefs will guide your decision-making and help you stay true to your vision. Take some time to reflect on what matters most to you and what you stand for.

With your goal and values in mind, it is time to set goals that align with your vision. These goals should be specific, measurable, and achievable. They should also be aligned with your values and beliefs. By setting clear and achievable goals, you will be able to track your progress and stay focused on your vision.

Finally, it is important to stay committed to your vision. This involves staying focused on your goals, overcoming obstacles, and staying true to your values and beliefs. Remember that success is not achieved overnight, but through hard work, dedication, and persistence.

Developing a personal vision is a crucial step in achieving success as an entrepreneur. By understanding what you want to achieve, defining your values and beliefs, setting clear and achievable goals, and staying committed to your vision, you will be able to overcome self-doubt and achieve success.

Building Resilience and Grit

and "Success".

As an entrepreneur, it's important to understand that success isn't achieved overnight. It's a journey that requires perseverance, resilience, and grit. Building resilience and grit is an essential component of achieving success as an entrepreneur. Resilience is the ability to bounce back from setbacks and adversity, while grit is the perseverance and passion to achieve long-term goals.

To build resilience and grit, it's important to adopt a growth mindset. A growth mindset is the belief that abilities and intelligence can be developed through dedication and hard work. People with a growth mindset are more likely to persist through challenges and setbacks, and to continue learning and growing.

In order to develop a growth mindset, it's important to embrace failure as a learning opportunity. Failure is an inevitable part of the entrepreneurial journey, but it's how you respond to failure that determines your success. Instead of giving up or dwelling on your mistakes, view them as opportunities to learn and grow.

Another way to build resilience and grit is to cultivate a strong support system. Surround yourself with people who believe in you and your vision, and who will support you through the ups and downs of entrepreneurship. This can include mentors, coaches, accountability partners, or a mastermind group.

Finally, it's important to take care of yourself both physically and mentally. Self-care can help you recharge and stay focused on your goals. This can include exercise, meditation, getting enough sleep, and taking breaks when needed.

Building resilience and grit is essential for achieving success as an entrepreneur. By adopting a growth mindset, embracing failure as a learning opportunity, cultivating a strong support system, and taking care of yourself, you can overcome self-doubt and achieve your goals. Remember, success is a journey, and building resilience and grit will help you stay the course.

The Power of Positive Affirmations

and "Achieving Success."

The Power of Positive Affirmations

As an entrepreneur, self-doubt can creep in at any time. It can sabotage your efforts, prevent you from taking risks, and hold you back from achieving success. But what if there was a way to combat self-doubt and boost your confidence and self-belief? The answer lies in the power of positive affirmations.

Positive affirmations are simple statements that you repeat to yourself on a regular basis. They are designed to help you shift your mindset from negative to positive, and to reinforce positive beliefs about yourself and your abilities. By repeating positive affirmations, you can reprogram your subconscious mind and create a more positive and empowering mindset.

The key to the effectiveness of positive affirmations is repetition. The more you repeat a positive affirmation, the more it becomes ingrained in your subconscious mind. Over time, you will start to believe the affirmation, and it will become a part of your internal dialogue. This can have a profound effect on your thoughts, emotions, and behaviors.

There are many different types of positive affirmations that you can use as an entrepreneur.

Some examples include:

- I am capable of achieving my goals.
- I am confident in my abilities.
- I am worthy of success.
- I am a successful entrepreneur.
- I am attracting abundance and prosperity.

To get the most out of positive affirmations, it is important to use them consistently and with intention.

Here are some tips for using positive affirmations effectively:

- Choose affirmations that resonate with you and your goals.
- Write your affirmations down and place them where you can see them regularly.
- Repeat your affirmations daily, ideally in the morning and before bed.
- Say your affirmations out loud and with conviction.
- Visualize yourself embodying the affirmations.

Incorporating positive affirmations into your daily routine can be a powerful tool for overcoming self-doubt and achieving success as an entrepreneur. By shifting your mindset from negative to positive, you can create a more empowering and confident version of yourself. So start incorporating positive affirmations into your routine today and watch as your mindset and success soar.

Practicing Mindfulness

Understanding Mindfulness and Its Benefits

and "Achieving Success."

Mindfulness is a term that's been thrown around a lot in recent years, but what does it actually mean, and why should entrepreneurs care about it? Put simply, mindfulness is the practice of being present and fully engaged in the current moment, without judgment or distraction. It's a way of training your mind to focus on what's happening right now, rather than getting caught up in worries about the past or future.

For entrepreneurs, practicing mindfulness can have a number of benefits. First and foremost, it can help you overcome self-doubt by allowing you to focus on the present moment rather than getting lost in negative thoughts about the future. This can be particularly helpful when facing challenges or setbacks, as it allows you to approach the situation with a clear and focused mind.

In addition to helping with self-doubt, mindfulness can also improve your overall well-being. Studies have shown that regular mindfulness practice can reduce stress and anxiety, improve sleep quality, and even boost immune function. As an entrepreneur, prioritizing your mental and physical health is essential to achieving success in the long-term.

So, how can you start incorporating mindfulness into your daily routine? One simple way is to set aside a few minutes each day for a mindful practice, such as meditation or deep breathing exercises. You can also try to bring mindfulness into your daily activities, such as eating or walking, by focusing on the sensations and experiences of the present moment.

Overall, understanding and practicing mindfulness can be a powerful tool for entrepreneurs looking to overcome self-doubt and achieve success. By training your mind to focus on the present moment, you can improve your overall well-being and approach challenges with a clear and focused mindset.

Mindfulness Techniques for Entrepreneurs

and "Achieving Success".

Mindfulness Techniques for Entrepreneurs

As an entrepreneur, it's natural to feel overwhelmed by the demands of running a business. The pressure to succeed can be intense, leading to self-doubt and anxiety. However, practicing mindfulness can help you overcome these negative emotions and achieve greater success.

Mindfulness is the practice of being fully present in the moment, without judgment. It's a powerful tool for entrepreneurs who want to improve their focus, reduce stress, and increase productivity. Here are some mindfulness techniques that can help you achieve these goals:

1. Meditation: Meditation is one of the best mindfulness techniques for entrepreneurs. It helps you calm your mind and focus your thoughts. Start by setting aside a few minutes each day to meditate. Sit in a quiet place, close your eyes, and focus on your breath. When your mind wanders, gently bring your attention back to your breath.

2. Gratitude: Gratitude is a powerful emotion that can help you overcome self-doubt and achieve success. Take a few minutes each day to reflect on the things you're grateful for in your life and business. This can help you shift your focus to the positive aspects of your life and business, rather than dwelling on the negative.

3. Mindful Movement: Mindful movement is another great mindfulness technique for entrepreneurs. It involves moving your body in a mindful way, such as through yoga or tai chi. This can help you reduce stress, improve your focus, and increase your energy levels.

4. Mindful Eating: Mindful eating is the practice of paying attention to your food while you eat. This can help you enjoy your food more, reduce overeating, and improve your digestion. Take a few minutes before each meal to focus on your food and appreciate the flavors and textures.

5. Mindful Breathing: Mindful breathing is a simple mindfulness technique that you can do anywhere, at any time. Simply focus on your breath, taking deep, slow breaths in and out. This can help you reduce stress, improve your focus, and increase your energy levels.

Practicing mindfulness can help you overcome self-doubt and achieve greater success as an entrepreneur. By incorporating these mindfulness techniques into your daily routine, you can improve your focus, reduce stress, and increase your productivity.

Using Mindfulness to Overcome Self-Doubt

Using Mindfulness to Overcome Self-Doubt

Self-doubt is a common challenge that entrepreneurs face on their journey to success. It can be a significant barrier to achieving your goals, as it can hold you back from taking the necessary risks and making the tough decisions that can propel your business forward. However, self-doubt is not a permanent state of being. With the right mindset and tools, you can overcome it and build the confidence necessary to achieve your goals.

One powerful tool for overcoming self-doubt is mindfulness. Mindfulness is the practice of being present in the moment, without judgment or distraction. It is a powerful way to quiet the noise of self-doubt and focus on the present moment. When you are mindful, you are better able to see your thoughts and emotions for what they are, without getting caught up in them. This can help you to be more objective and less reactive, which can help you to overcome self-doubt.

To practice mindfulness, it is helpful to start with a few simple techniques. One effective technique is to focus on your breath. As you inhale and exhale, pay attention to the sensations in your body. Notice the rise and fall of your chest, the feeling of air moving in and out of your nostrils, and the rhythm of your breath. If your mind starts to wander, gently bring your focus back to your breath. By practicing this technique regularly, you can train your mind to be more focused and less distracted.

Another effective mindfulness technique is to practice gratitude. This involves taking a few moments each day to reflect on the things you are grateful for. This can be anything from the people in your life to the opportunities you have been given. When you focus on the positive aspects of your life, you are less likely to get caught up in negative thoughts and emotions.

Mindfulness is a powerful tool for overcoming self-doubt. By practicing mindfulness techniques regularly, you can train your mind to be more focused and less reactive. This can help you to overcome self-doubt and build the confidence necessary to achieve your goals. So, if you are struggling with self-doubt, try incorporating mindfulness into your daily routine. With practice, you will find that it becomes easier to quiet the noise of self-doubt and focus on the present moment.

Developing a Growth Mindset

Understanding the Difference between Fixed and Growth Mindset

and "Achieving Success".

As entrepreneurs, it is important to understand the difference between having a fixed mindset and a growth mindset. Your mindset can determine the level of success you will achieve in your business. A fixed mindset is one where you believe that your abilities and intelligence are fixed and cannot be altered. You believe that you are born with a certain level of intelligence and talent, and that is all you will ever have. People with a fixed mindset tend to avoid challenges, give up easily, and are afraid of failure. This mindset can limit your potential for growth and success.

On the other hand, a growth mindset is one where you believe that your abilities and intelligence can be developed through hard work, dedication, and perseverance. You view challenges as opportunities to learn and grow, and you embrace failure as a necessary part of the learning process. People with a growth mindset are more likely to take risks, persist in the face of obstacles, and achieve higher levels of success.

To develop a growth mindset, you need to start by recognizing the beliefs and attitudes that are holding you back. Begin by challenging your fixed beliefs and adopting a more positive and growth-oriented mindset. Start by embracing challenges and viewing them as opportunities to learn and grow. Instead of giving up easily, persevere and try new approaches until you achieve the desired outcome.

Another important factor in developing a growth mindset is to surround yourself with positive and supportive people who will encourage and motivate you. Seek out mentors and coaches who can help you develop your skills and provide guidance and support as you work towards achieving your goals.

Understanding the difference between a fixed and growth mindset is crucial for entrepreneurs who want to achieve success in their businesses. By adopting a growth mindset, you can overcome self-doubt and achieve your full potential. Remember, success is not determined by your innate abilities, but by your willingness to work hard, learn, and grow.

How to Develop a Growth Mindset

and "Achieving Success."

As an entrepreneur, having a growth mindset is crucial for success. A growth mindset is the belief that one's abilities and intelligence can be developed through dedication and hard work. This mindset encourages individuals to embrace challenges, learn from failures, and persist in the face of setbacks.

Here are some tips for developing a growth mindset:

1. Embrace challenges

Instead of avoiding challenges, embrace them as opportunities for growth. Challenges help you develop new skills and expand your knowledge. When faced with a challenge, ask yourself what you can learn from it and how you can improve.

2. Learn from failures

Failure is a natural part of the learning process. Instead of viewing failure as a setback, see it as an opportunity to learn and grow. Reflect on what went wrong and how you can improve next time. Remember that every successful entrepreneur has experienced failure at some point.

3. Cultivate a love of learning

Successful entrepreneurs never stop learning. They are constantly seeking new knowledge and skills to improve their businesses. Cultivate a love of learning by reading books, attending seminars, and seeking out mentors. Remember that knowledge is power in the business world.

4. Stay positive

A positive attitude is essential for developing a growth mindset. Instead of focusing on your weaknesses, focus on your strengths and what you can do to improve. Surround yourself with positive, supportive people who will encourage and motivate you.

5. Persist in the face of setbacks

Entrepreneurship is not easy, and setbacks are inevitable. However, a growth mindset encourages individuals to persist in the face of adversity. Remember that success is not achieved overnight, and that persistence and dedication are key to achieving your goals.

By developing a growth mindset, entrepreneurs can overcome self-doubt and achieve success. Embrace challenges, learn from failures, cultivate a love of learning, stay positive, and persist in the face of setbacks. With these tips, you can develop a growth mindset and achieve your entrepreneurial dreams.

The Benefits of a Growth Mindset for Entrepreneurs

and "Achieving Success".

The Benefits of a Growth Mindset for Entrepreneurs

Entrepreneurship is not for the faint of heart. It takes courage, resilience, and a strong sense of purpose to succeed in the competitive and often unpredictable world of business. However, one of the most important factors that can determine an entrepreneur's success is their mindset.

A growth mindset is the belief that intelligence, talent, and abilities can be developed through hard work, dedication, and persistence. This mindset is in contrast to a fixed mindset, which is the belief that intelligence and talent are innate and cannot be changed.

For entrepreneurs, a growth mindset can provide numerous benefits that can help them overcome self-doubt and achieve success. **Here are some of the most significant benefits of a growth mindset for entrepreneurs:**

1. Embracing Challenges

Entrepreneurs face numerous challenges on their journey to success, from raising capital to developing a product or service that meets the needs of their target market. A growth mindset allows entrepreneurs to view these challenges as opportunities to grow and learn, rather than insurmountable obstacles.

2. Resilience

Entrepreneurship is full of ups and downs, and setbacks are inevitable. A growth mindset allows entrepreneurs to bounce back from setbacks and failures quickly, learning from their mistakes and using them as opportunities for growth.

3. Creativity

A growth mindset encourages entrepreneurs to think outside the box and come up with innovative solutions to problems. Rather than being bound by conventional thinking, entrepreneurs with a growth mindset are more likely to take risks and try new things.

4. Continuous Learning

Entrepreneurs with a growth mindset are committed to continuous learning and self-improvement. They seek out new knowledge and skills, and are open to feedback and constructive criticism.

5. Persistence

Entrepreneurship requires persistence and determination. A growth mindset allows entrepreneurs to stay motivated and focused on their goals, even when faced with obstacles or setbacks.

In conclusion, a growth mindset is essential for entrepreneurs who want to overcome self-doubt and achieve success. By embracing challenges, being resilient, fostering creativity, committing to continuous learning, and staying persistent, entrepreneurs with a growth mindset can achieve great things and make a positive impact in the world.

Overcoming Failure and Setbacks

Understanding Failure and Resilience

and "Achieving Success".

Failure and resilience are two sides of the same coin. Every entrepreneur has faced failure at some point in their journey, whether it be a failed product launch, a rejected pitch, or a financial setback. However, the ability to bounce back from these failures is what separates successful entrepreneurs from the rest.

It is crucial for entrepreneurs to understand that failure is not the end, but rather a stepping stone towards success. Failure is inevitable in any venture, but it should not be seen as a reflection of one's abilities or worth. Instead, it should be viewed as a valuable learning experience that can provide insights into what went wrong and how to improve in the future.

Resilience, on the other hand, is the ability to recover quickly from setbacks and adapt to changing circumstances. It is a trait that can be developed through practice and mindset. Resilient entrepreneurs are those who do not give up easily and are willing to persevere through challenges.

One way to cultivate resilience is by adopting a growth mindset. This mindset is characterized by a belief that abilities and intelligence can be developed through hard work and dedication. Entrepreneurs with a growth mindset are more likely to see failures as opportunities for growth and improvement, rather than as a reflection of their abilities.

Another way to build resilience is by seeking support from others. Entrepreneurs can benefit from having a strong network of mentors, advisors, and peers who can provide guidance and encouragement during tough times. Additionally, seeking feedback from customers and stakeholders can help entrepreneurs identify areas for improvement and make necessary adjustments to their business strategies.

By embracing failure as a learning experience and cultivating resilience through a growth mindset and support from others, entrepreneurs can bounce back from setbacks and continue to move forward on their journey towards success.

Learning from Failure and Moving Forward

and "Achieving Success".

Learning from Failure and Moving Forward

As an entrepreneur, failure is a part of the journey towards success. It is inevitable and should be embraced as a learning opportunity. Failure can be a hard pill to swallow, especially when you have invested so much time, energy, and resources into a project or business venture. However, it's important to remember that failure is not the end of the road. It's just a detour that can lead to greater success if you choose to learn from it.

One of the keys to overcoming self-doubt and achieving success is to have a growth mindset. People with a growth mindset see failure as a learning opportunity and a chance to improve. They embrace challenges and see them as opportunities to grow and develop. This mindset helps entrepreneurs to move forward after a setback, equipped with knowledge and experience that they can use to do better next time.

To learn from failure, entrepreneurs need to be honest with themselves about what went wrong. They should evaluate their actions and decisions, identify the mistakes they made, and take responsibility for them. This process requires humility and a willingness to learn from others. It's important to seek feedback from mentors, advisors, and colleagues who can provide constructive criticism and help you identify areas for improvement.

Once you have identified the lessons to be learned from failure, it's important to take action. Entrepreneurs should use the knowledge gained to make changes and improve their strategies. This might involve pivoting your business model, refining your marketing strategy, or investing in staff training. The key is to take action and use the lessons learned to move forward.

Failure is an inevitable part of the entrepreneurial journey. Successful entrepreneurs are those who embrace failure as a learning opportunity, adopt a growth mindset, and use the lessons learned to improve their strategies. By learning from failure and moving forward, you can overcome self-doubt and achieve success in your business ventures.

Overcoming Setbacks and Challenges

and "Achieving Success".

Overcoming Setbacks and Challenges

As an entrepreneur, setbacks and challenges are inevitable. No matter how well you plan, there will always be unexpected obstacles along the way. However, it's important to remember that setbacks and challenges are not failures, they are opportunities to learn and grow.

The first step in overcoming setbacks and challenges is to adopt a growth mindset. This means seeing failures as opportunities to learn and improve, rather than as a reflection of your worth as a person or entrepreneur. With a growth mindset, setbacks become stepping stones to success.

One of the keys to overcoming setbacks and challenges is resilience. Resilience is the ability to bounce back from adversity and keep moving forward. It's not about never experiencing setbacks or failures, but about how you respond to them. Resilient entrepreneurs are able to adapt to change, stay focused on their goals, and keep pushing forward even in the face of adversity.

Another important factor in overcoming setbacks and challenges is perseverance. Perseverance is the ability to keep going even when things get tough. It's about staying committed to your goals and not giving up, even when it feels like the odds are against you. Successful entrepreneurs understand that setbacks and challenges are part of the journey, and they have the perseverance to keep pushing through until they achieve their goals.

Finally, it's important to have a support system in place. This can include mentors, coaches, friends, and family members who believe in you and your vision. When you're facing setbacks and challenges, having a support system can make all the difference. They can offer encouragement, advice, and a fresh perspective that can help you overcome obstacles and stay focused on your goals.

Setbacks and challenges are an inevitable part of the entrepreneurial journey. However, with a growth mindset, resilience, perseverance, and a strong support system, you can overcome any obstacle and achieve success. Remember, setbacks are not failures, they are opportunities to learn and grow. Keep pushing forward and never give up on your dreams.

Navigating the Entrepreneurial Journey

The Importance of Goal Setting

and "Achieving Success".

The Importance of Goal Setting

As an entrepreneur, setting goals is crucial to your success. Without clear objectives, it becomes difficult to measure progress and track success. Goal setting is a fundamental aspect of mindset mastery that can help you overcome self-doubt and achieve the success you desire.

Goal setting allows you to define your vision and establish a clear path towards achieving it. When you have a clear understanding of what you want to achieve, you can break down your goals into smaller, more manageable tasks that can be accomplished in a timely manner. This helps to create a sense of progress and accomplishment, which boosts your confidence and motivates you to keep going.

Setting goals also helps you to stay focused and avoid distractions. When you have a clear understanding of what you want to achieve, it becomes easier to prioritize your actions and avoid activities that do not contribute to your goals. This helps to reduce feelings of overwhelm and increase productivity, which ultimately leads to success.

Moreover, goal setting helps you to stay accountable. When you set goals, you are making a commitment to yourself to achieve them. This creates a sense of responsibility that keeps you motivated and focused on taking the necessary actions to achieve your goals. It also helps you to measure progress and adjust your strategies if necessary, which ultimately leads to success.

Goal setting helps you to define your vision, stay focused, stay accountable, and measure progress. By setting clear and achievable goals, you can overcome self-doubt and achieve the success you desire. Remember, goal setting is a fundamental aspect of mindset mastery that can transform your life and business.

Staying Focused and Motivated

and "Achieving Success".

Staying Focused and Motivated

Entrepreneurship is a challenging journey that requires a lot of hard work, dedication, and sacrifices. As an entrepreneur, you must stay focused and motivated to overcome the various obstacles that come your way. In this subchapter, we will explore some practical tips that can help you stay focused and motivated on your entrepreneurial journey.

Set Goals and Priorities

The first step to staying focused and motivated is to set clear goals and priorities. Identify what you want to achieve, and break down your goals into smaller, achievable tasks. Prioritize your tasks based on their importance and urgency. This will help you to stay on track and avoid getting overwhelmed by the various demands of entrepreneurship.

Create a Schedule

Creating a schedule is another effective way to stay focused and motivated. Plan your day, week, or month in advance, and allocate specific times for your tasks. This will help you to manage your time effectively and avoid procrastination. Stick to your schedule as much as possible and avoid distractions that can derail your progress.

Surround Yourself with Positive Influences

Surrounding yourself with positive influences is crucial for staying motivated and focused. Seek out mentors, coaches, and peers who share your vision and can provide you with guidance and support. Join networking groups, attend conferences, and participate in online communities to connect with like-minded individuals who can inspire and motivate you.

Celebrate Your Successes

Celebrating your successes, no matter how small, is an essential aspect of staying motivated and focused. Acknowledge and appreciate your accomplishments, and use them as a source of inspiration to keep pushing forward. Remember that entrepreneurship is a journey, and every milestone is worth celebrating.

Set clear goals, create a schedule, surround yourself with positive influences, and celebrate your successes. These tips can help you stay on track and motivated on your entrepreneurial journey.

Embracing Change and Managing Uncertainty

and "Achieving Success."

Embracing Change and Managing Uncertainty

As an entrepreneur, you are no stranger to change and uncertainty. In fact, these two aspects of business are arguably some of the most challenging to navigate. However, with the right mindset, you can not only embrace change, but also manage the uncertainty that comes with it.

One of the keys to embracing change is to adopt a growth mindset. This is the belief that you can learn, grow, and develop your skills through effort and persistence. With a growth mindset, you see challenges as opportunities to learn and improve, rather than obstacles to be avoided.

Another important aspect of embracing change is to stay open to new ideas and perspectives. As an entrepreneur, you are constantly seeking out new opportunities and solutions. By remaining open to different viewpoints, you can gain valuable insights and adapt your approach accordingly.

Managing uncertainty also requires a certain mindset. Specifically, it requires a willingness to take calculated risks. This means that you are willing to take a chance on a new idea or opportunity, but only after carefully evaluating the potential risks and rewards.

Another key to managing uncertainty is to focus on what you can control. While there are many factors that are outside of your control, there are also many things that you can influence. By focusing on these controllable factors, you can take proactive steps to mitigate risk and increase your chances of success.

Finally, it is important to remember that uncertainty is a natural part of entrepreneurship. While it can be unsettling at times, it is also what makes the journey so rewarding. By embracing change and managing uncertainty, you can continue to grow and thrive as an entrepreneur, overcoming self-doubt and achieving success.

Conclusion

Recap of Key Takeaways

and "Achieving Success".

Recap of Key Takeaways:

Mindset Mastery for Entrepreneurs: Overcoming Self-Doubt and Achieving Success is a book that is designed to help entrepreneurs overcome their self-doubt and achieve success in their businesses. Throughout the book, various key takeaways have been highlighted, and it is essential that entrepreneurs pay attention to these takeaways as they will help them to grow and succeed in their businesses.

#1 The importance of having a growth mindset. This mindset is essential for entrepreneurs because it allows them to approach challenges with a positive attitude and a willingness to learn. With a growth mindset, entrepreneurs are more likely to take risks, which can lead to greater success.

#2 The importance of taking action. Many entrepreneurs get stuck in analysis paralysis, and they never take the necessary steps to move their businesses forward. To overcome this, entrepreneurs should focus on taking small, actionable steps towards their goals every day.

#3 The importance of surrounding oneself with positive influences. Entrepreneurs should seek out mentors, coaches, and other successful entrepreneurs who can offer guidance and support. Additionally, entrepreneurs should avoid negative influences that can bring them down and make them doubt themselves.

#4 The importance of perseverance. Entrepreneurship is a challenging journey, and setbacks are inevitable. However, entrepreneurs who are determined to succeed will persevere through these setbacks and come out stronger on the other side.

#5 The importance of self-care. Entrepreneurs often neglect their physical and mental health in pursuit of their business goals. However, taking care of oneself is essential for long-term success. Entrepreneurs should prioritize getting enough sleep, eating a healthy diet, exercising regularly, and taking breaks to recharge.

These five key points of Mindset Mastery can help entrepreneurs overcome their self-doubt and achieve success in their businesses. By adopting a growth mindset, taking action, surrounding oneself with positive influences, persevering through setbacks, and practicing self-care, entrepreneurs can build successful businesses that they can be proud of.

Final Thoughts and Encouragement

and "Achieving Success".

Final Thoughts and Encouragement

Congratulations! You have made it to the end of this book, which means you have taken the first step towards mastering your mindset as an entrepreneur. You have learned about the importance of having a growth mindset, how to overcome self-doubt, and the habits that successful entrepreneurs have in common. However, this is just the beginning of your journey towards success.

Remember that it is okay to make mistakes and fail. In fact, failure is an essential part of the learning process. It is through failure that we learn what does not work and what we need to improve on. Do not let fear of failure hold you back from taking risks and trying new things.

Surround yourself with like-minded individuals who will support you and encourage you. Join a community of entrepreneurs, attend networking events, and seek out mentors who have achieved the level of success you aspire to. Learn from their experiences and insights.

Stay focused on your goals and keep pushing forward. It is easy to become distracted by the daily challenges and setbacks that come with entrepreneurship, but do not lose sight of your vision. Visualize your success and keep working towards it.

Finally, remember that success is not just about achieving financial wealth or recognition. It is about finding fulfillment in what you do and making a positive impact on the world. Use your skills and resources to give back to your community and create a better future for everyone.

Mastering your mindset as an entrepreneur is a continuous process. It requires self-awareness, perseverance, and a willingness to learn and grow. Keep these principles in mind and continue to develop your growth mindset. You have the potential to achieve great things, so go out there and make it happen.

Resources for Further Learning and Growth.

and "Achieving Success."

As an entrepreneur, it's essential to have a growth mindset and constantly seek out resources for learning and growth. Fortunately, there are many resources available to help you overcome self-doubt and achieve success. Here are some of the best resources for further learning and growth:

1. Books: Reading books is one of the best ways to gain new knowledge and skills. There are many great books on entrepreneurship, self-improvement, and personal development. Some of the best books include "The Lean Startup" by Eric Ries, "The 7 Habits of Highly Effective People" by Stephen Covey, and "Think and Grow Rich" by Napoleon Hill.

2. Podcasts: Podcasts are a great way to learn on the go. There are many great podcasts on entrepreneurship, self-improvement, and personal development. Some of the best podcasts include "Entrepreneur on Fire" by John Lee Dumas, "The Tim Ferriss Show" by Tim Ferriss, and "The School of Greatness" by Lewis Howes.

3. Online courses: There are many great online courses available to help you learn new skills and gain new knowledge. Some of the best online courses include Udemy, Coursera, and Lynda.com.

4. Mentors: Having a mentor can be incredibly valuable for entrepreneurs. A mentor can provide guidance, advice, and support as you navigate the challenges of entrepreneurship. You can find mentors through networking events, online communities, and professional organizations.

5. Mastermind groups: A mastermind group is a group of like-minded individuals who come together to support each other and share ideas. Joining a mastermind group can be a great way to gain new insights and perspectives on your business.

6. Conferences and events: Attending conferences and events can be a great way to learn from experts and network with other entrepreneurs. Some of the best conferences and events include the Entrepreneur Summit, the Small Business Expo, and the Inc. 500|5000 Conference.

In conclusion, as an entrepreneur, it's important to have a growth mindset and constantly seek out resources for learning and growth. Whether it's reading books, listening to podcasts, taking online courses, finding mentors, joining mastermind groups, or attending conferences and events, there are many resources available to help you overcome self-doubt and achieve success.

www.ingramcontent.com/pod-product-compliance
Lightning Source LLC
Chambersburg PA
CBHW040331220526
45473CB00009B/2647